SOME MAJOR EVENTS IN WORLD WAR II

THE EUROPEAN THEATER

1939 SEPTEMBER—Germany invades Poland Great Britain, France, Australia, & New Zealand declare war on Germany; Battle of the Atlantic begins. NOVEMBER—Russia invades Finland.

1940 APRIL—Germany invades Denmark & Norway. MAY—Germany invades Belgium, Luxembourg, & The Netherlands; British forces retreat to Dunkirk and escape to England. JUNE—Italy declares war on Britain & France; France surrenders to Germany. JULY—Battle of Britain begins. SEPTEMBER—Italy invades Egypt; Germany, Italy, & Japan form the Axis countries. OCTOBER—Italy invades Greece. NOVEMBER—Battle of Britain over. DECEMBER—Britain attacks Italy in North Africa.

1941 JANUARY—Allies take Tobruk. FEBRUARY—Rommel arrives at Tripoli. APRIL—Germany invades Greece & Yugoslavia. JUNE—Allies are in Syria; Germany invades Russia. JULY—Russia joins Allies. AUGUST—Germans capture Kiev. OCTOBER—Germany reaches Moscow. DECEMBER—Germans retreat from Moscow; Japan attacks Pearl Harbor; United States enters war against Axis nations.

1942 MAY—first British bomber attack on Cologne. JUNE—Germans take Tobruk. SEPTEMBER—Battle of Stalingrad begins. OCTOBER—Battle of El Alamein begins. NOVEMBER—Allies recapture Tobruk; Russians counterattack at Stalingrad.

1943 JANUARY—Allies take Tripoli. FEBRUARY—German troops at Stalingrad surrender. APRIL—revolt of Warsaw Ghetto Jews begins. MAY—German and Italian resistance in North Africa is over; their troops surrender in Tunisia; Warsaw Ghetto revolt is put down by Germany. JULY—allies invade Sicily; Mussolini put in prison. SEPTEMBER—Allies land in Italy; Italians surrender; Germans occupy Rome; Mussolini rescued by Germany. OCTOBER—Allies capture Naples; Italy declares war on Germany. NOVEMBER—Russians recapture Kiev.

1944 JANUARY—Allies land at Anzio. JUNE—Rome falls to Allies; Allies land in Normandy (D-Day). JULY—assassination attempt on Hitler fails. AUGUST—Allies land in southern France. SEPTEMBER—Brussels freed. OCTOBER—Athens liberated. DECEMBER—Battle of the Bulge.

1945 JANUARY—Russians free Warsaw. FEBRUARY—Dresden bombed. APRIL—Americans take Belsen and Buchenwald concentration camps Russians free Vienna; Russians take over Berlin Mussolini killed; Hitler commits suicide. MAY—Germany surrenders; Goering captured.

THE PACIFIC THEATER

1940 SEPTEMBER—Japan joins Axis nations Germany & Italy.

1941 APRIL—Russia & Japan sign neutrality pact DECEMBER—Japanese launch attacks against Pearl Harbor, Hong Kong, the Philippines, & Malaya United States and Allied nations declare war on Japan; China declares war on Japan, Germany, & Italy Japan takes over Guam, Wake Island, & Hong Kong; Japan attacks Burma.

1942 JANUARY—Japan takes over Manila; Japan invades Dutch East Indies. FEBRUARY—Japan takes over Singapore; Battle of the Java Sea. APRIL—Japanese overrun Bataan. MAY—Japan takes Mandalay; Allied forces in Philippines surrender to Japan; Japan takes Corregidor; Battle of the Coral Sea. JUNE—Battle of Midway; Japan occupies Aleutian Islands. AUGUST—United States invades Guadalcanal in the Solomon Islands.

1943 FEBRUARY—Guadalcanal taken by U.S. Marines. MARCH—Japanese begin to retreat in China. APRIL—Yamamoto shot down by U.S. Air Force. MAY—U.S. troops take Aleutian Islands back from Japan. JUNE—Allied troops land in New Guinea. NOVEMBER—U.S. Marines invade Bougainville & Tarawa.

1944 FEBRUARY—Truk liberated. JUNE—Saipan attacked by United States. JULY—battle for Guam begins. OCTOBER—U.S. troops invade Philippines Battle of Leyte Gulf won by Allies.

1945 JANUARY—Luzon taken; Burma Road won back. MARCH—Iwo Jima freed. APRIL—Okinawa attacked by U.S. troops; President Franklin Roosevelt dies; Harry S. Truman becomes president JUNE—United States takes Okinawa. AUGUST—atomic bomb dropped on Hiroshima; Russia declares war on Japan; atomic bomb dropped on Nagasaki. SEPTEMBER—Japan surrenders.

WORLD AT WAR

Battle of the Atlantic

WORLD AT WAR

Battle of the Atlantic

By G. C. Skipper

CHILDRENS PRESS, CHICAGO

A smoking room on the British liner *Athenia*

FRONTISPIECE:
A German drawing of a depth-charge attack on a U-boat

PROJECT EDITOR
Joan Downing

CREATIVE DIRECTOR
Margrit Fiddle

Library of Congress Cataloging in Publication Data

Skipper, G.C.
   Battle of the Atlantic.

   (World at war)
   SUMMARY: Describes the struggle for control
of the Atlantic Ocean during World War II.
   1. World War, 1939-1945—Atlantic Ocean—
Juvenile literature. [1. World War, 1939-1945—
Atlantic Ocean] I. Title. II. Series: Skipper,
G.C. World at war
D770.S48   940.54'29   81-6186
ISBN 0-516-04793-0   AACR2

PICTURE CREDITS:
UPI: Cover, pages 4, 6, 9, 10, 11, 13, 14,
17, 19 (bottom pictures), 20, 23, 24, 25,
27, 29, 31, 42 (bottom), 43 (top and
center), 45, 46
NATIONAL ARCHIVES: pages 12, 16, 19
(top), 32, 35, 38, 39, 40, 42 (top and
center), 43 (bottom), 44
LEN MEENTS: pages 36-37 (map)

COVER PHOTO:
A convoy in the North Atlantic

The British liner *Athenia* glided gracefully through the water. She was sailing across the Atlantic and making excellent time. Aboard were 1,400 passengers, including many Americans. A few had been seasick, but most were trying to enjoy the luxury of their journey. Lights burned brightly throughout the ship. Passengers relaxed in cabins, lounges, and in the dining rooms. A few brave souls strolled along the decks in the cool, damp, night air.

The date was September 3, 1939. That very morning Great Britain had declared war on Nazi Germany. Two days earlier—at dawn on September 1—Germany had invaded Poland, one of Britain's allies. German dictator Adolf Hitler had ignored Britain's demand that the invasion be halted. Now Poland, Great Britain, and France were at war with Nazi Germany. The entire world was watching Hitler in fear and anger. No one knew exactly how far he would go.

But many of the people aboard the *Athenia* had had enough of war talk. They were uneasy, but wanted to enjoy the cruise. The ship was full of laughter and small talk.

"Is it true that these waters are becoming dangerous?" a woman in an evening gown asked her companion. "Do you think we are safe?"

"Oh, don't be melodramatic," the man replied. "Of course we're safe. We're not on a military ship, you know."

The woman laughed a little nervously. She glanced around the room, then turned again to her companion. "Well, if you say so," she said. "What time is it, by the way?"

The man looked at his watch. "Nearly nine o'clock," he answered. "It's too early to return to the cabin. The night is still young!"

A few minutes later there was a great explosion. Without any warning, a German submarine had fired a torpedo. It had sliced silently across the water directly at the *Athenia*. The submarine disappeared beneath the water and was gone.

SUN DECK
PROMENADE
A DECK
B DECK
C DECK

The *Athenia*

Behind it lay the stricken *Athenia* and 112 bodies. Twenty-eight of those killed were Americans.

The Battle of the Atlantic—and World War II—had begun in earnest.

German submarines had been a menace during World War I. Now they were back in action. They were known as U-boats, a contraction of *Unterseebooten*, the German word for submarines. German U-boats and surface ships were about to wage a vicious battle against the British in the Atlantic Ocean.

German victories came fast at first. On September 17, 1939, a U-boat off the southwest coast of Ireland opened fire on the British aircraft carrier *Courageous*. The British ship went down with 500 men.

Ten days later, two great German battleships, the *Graf Spee* and the *Deutschland*, began their campaign against British shipping. During the next three months, the *Graf Spee* alone sank nine British cargo vessels.

The German battleships *Deutschland* (right) and *Graf Spee* (below) are shown as they looked before the war.

Above: The eleven-inch guns of the *Deutschland* fire a broadside.
Below: This picture, taken from the deck of the *Graf Spee*, shows one of her victims sinking in the Atlantic.

On October 14, 1939, the British sustained a
bitter blow. Their battleship *Royal Oak* was
anchored at Scapa Flow, a supposedly safe
harbor. Scapa Flow was the British naval base
off the northern coast of Scotland. Its defenses
included a barrier of sunken ships and steel nets,
floating mines and depth charges. In addition,
patrolling British destroyers were equipped with
asdic. This was an underwater detection device
similar to sonar. It would register the presence of
enemy submarines.

Nevertheless, Commander Gunther Prien's
submarine, the *U-47*, somehow managed to sneak
through the barriers—unharmed and undetected.
In a daring and dangerous run, Prien had brought

Commander Prien was hailed as a hero on his return to Germany after sinking the British battleship *Royal Oak* in Scapa Flow.

the *U-47* to the very home of the British navy. There, under a sky blazing with the light of the aurora borealis, she surfaced. Incredibly, she still was not noticed. The *U-47* struck at her target. The *Royal Oak* was blown to bits and 786 men were killed.

Again, with amazing skill—and luck—Prien took his submarine back through the British defenses. The *U-47* was pursued by a British destroyer. She was attacked from the shore. She was attacked by gunboats and cruisers. And she was fighting the deadly strong current. Prien thought he was finished. But, miraculously, he brought the *U-47* through and escaped into the open ocean.

Above: The scuttled *Graf Spee* in flames. Below: The coffin of one of the Nazi seamen killed during the sea battle is lifted to the dock in Montevideo. Other coffins are covered by a swastika.

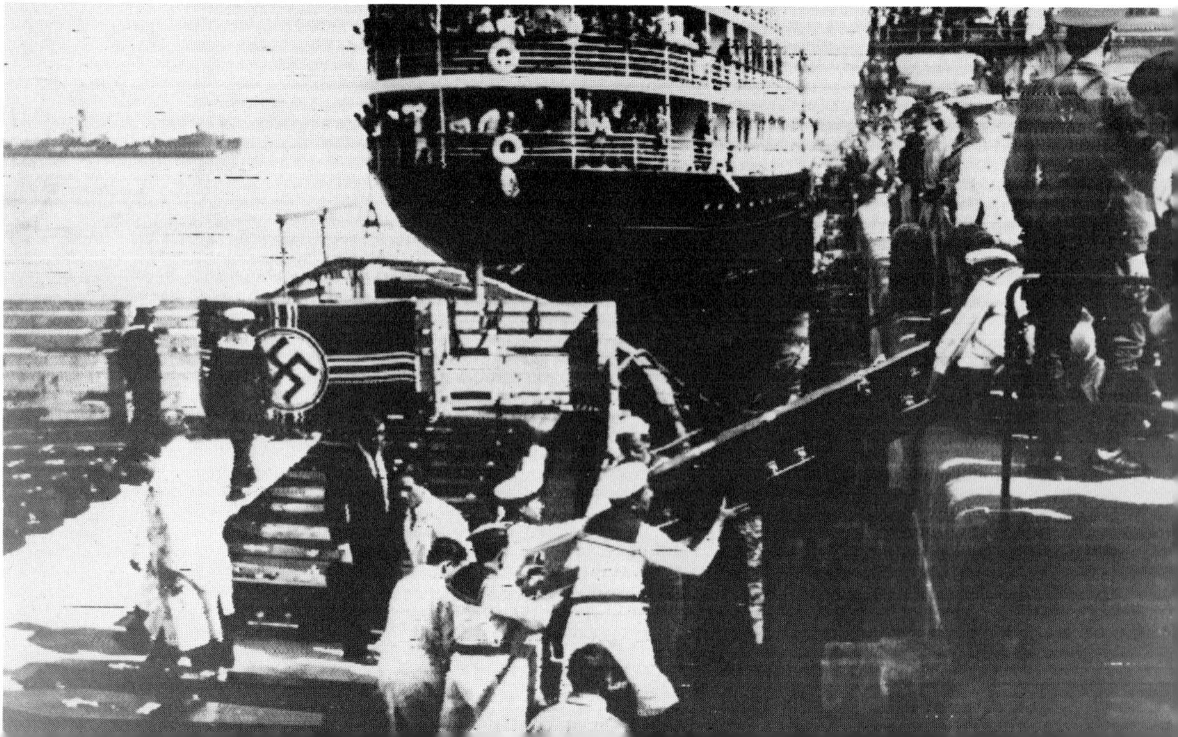

But not all incidents in the Atlantic resulted in German victories. In December of 1939, the *Graf Spee* tangled with three British cruisers in the South Atlantic. Guns roared across the water and smoke billowed skyward. Suddenly, the German ship was hit. The British cruisers *Exeter*, *Ajax*, and *Achilles* continued to blast away. The *Graf Spee* was in deep trouble. Though limping, she managed to pull away.

The *Graf Spee* escaped the British, but was badly damaged. She managed to make it to Montevideo, Uruguay, for repairs. But she would be permitted to remain in those neutral waters for only a short time. There was no way the ship could be ready for battle that quickly. And waiting outside the harbor were the *Ajax* and the *Achilles*. They had followed the German ship to Montevideo.

The *Graf Spee* wouldn't have a chance if she left the safety of the harbor. So Captain Hans Langsdorff scuttled the mighty ship. He took his crew up the Plate River to Buenos Aires, Argentina. There, unwilling to face the wrath of Hitler, he shot himself in a small hotel room.

During the six months between September 3, 1939, and February 29, 1940, Allied ships were being sunk by U-boats faster than they could be replaced. By the time the first year of war in the Atlantic was over, the British were sure of one thing. U-boats were dangerous. They operated with speed, silence, cleverness, and deadliness. It is no wonder they were called Grey Wolves.

There was no doubt that the man in command of the U-boats was brilliant. That man was Rear Admiral Karl Doenitz. Before the war in the Atlantic was over, Doenitz would replace Grand Admiral Erich Raeder as head of the entire German navy. Doenitz, however, would continue to command the U-boat operations.

Rear Admiral Karl Doenitz

Grand Admiral Erich Raeder

Left: A British cruiser goes down after being attacked by a German destroyer. Below: Though U-boats sank hundreds of Allied ships, their crews were men of honor. Whenever possible, they summoned help to rescue survivors of their attacks. This U-boat crew cheers as a Norwegian freighter answers their request to pick up the crew of a torpedoed tanker.

The German navy had a double mission in the Atlantic: stop British convoys from transporting war supplies and food to the United Kingdom, and sink British ships faster than they could be replaced. If British supply lines dried up, Nazi Germany could easily defeat hungry, poorly armed Great Britain.

During the third week of September, 1940, more British ships were sunk than in any other week of the war. But even though that week was the worst for the British since the Battle of the Atlantic had begun, losses were to get worse.

The following month, Admiral Doenitz introduced a new fighting tactic. He was desperately short of submarines and needed a way to use the few he had efficiently. Thus, the "wolf pack" was born. When a U-boat sighted an enemy convoy, the position of the convoy would be given to all nearby U-boats. They would speed to the location and attack the convoy from all sides. When they had done their damage, they would scatter in different directions.

Using the wolf-pack tactic, German U-boats sank more and more enemy vessels. Instead of losing only one or two ships in a convoy, the British were now losing several. In that month of October, 1940, twenty ships from a single British convoy were sunk by a wolf pack.

As word of the wolf packs spread, the British tried to figure out how to defend the convoys. Asdic was useless unless the submarines were under water and within range. Once the U-boats surfaced, asdic could not detect them.

Above: War flags are hoisted over a group of U-boats at Kiel. Below left: A Nazi U-boat commander relaxes after a battle as his chief mate (with pipe) leans over to speak with him. Below right: A Nazi submarine returns in triumph to its base. Each horseshoe pennant represents an enemy ship sunk by the U-boat.

The German battleships *Gniesenau* (shown above when she was launched in 1936) and the *Scharnhorst* (below) sank or captured many British ships during the Battle of the Atlantic.

The most obvious defense would be to spot a U-boat as it shadowed a convoy. But the U-boats usually stayed under water during the day and surfaced to attack only at night.

So the British came up with rockets called "snowflakes." They could change the darkness of night to the brightness of day. Several snowflakes sent up from ships in a convoy would light up the entire area. The U-boats would be clearly visible targets.

There was a drawback to this tactic, however. The ships in the convoy also would be good targets for the U-boats.

Radar had been very effective on land. The British now worked hard to figure out a way to improve radar's effectiveness on the sea. They *had* to find better ways to counteract the U-boat threat.

In the meantime, the year 1941 was hard on the British. The U-boats were not the only threat. Four German battleships—the *Hipper*, *Scharnhorst*, *Gneisenau*, and *Scheer*—also were creating havoc. These four ships sank or captured 40 British ships in only a few short months.

But by May of 1941, the British were no longer alone in their effort to keep the shipping lanes open. American ships had begun to bring badly needed supplies to Britain. They were also escorting British convoys.

Hitler was not ready for war with the United States. He refused to permit his navy to attack American ships. This situation was very frustrating for the German navy. Raeder pleaded with Hitler. He told him that some American ships had even joined in some of the sea battles against the Germans. It was bad enough that Americans were carrying supplies to the enemy and were protecting their convoys. But it was humiliating for the Germans to be prevented from defending themselves when they were fired upon by them!

The German leader remained firm. No German ship was to fire on an American ship—even in self defense.

The huge German battleship *Bismarck* was launched on February 14, 1939 (left), but it was more than two years before she was ready to enter the Battle of the Atlantic.

Then, on May 21, 1941, a German U-boat "accidentally" sank an American freighter, the *Robin Moor*. Hitler was furious. The *Robin Moor* hadn't even been in the German blockade zone. Hitler again warned Admiral Raeder that the navy was not to attack American vessels.

On the same day the *Robin Moor* was sunk, the British received some frightening news. They learned that the huge new German battleship *Bismarck* had been launched. That ship was more powerful than any other ship on the seas. The

Bismarck was heavily armored to protect herself from Allied torpedoes and bombs. She had eight huge 15-inch guns that could blow nearly anything out of the water. She also carried six airplanes. With her was the new cruiser *Prinz Eugen.*

The British could not allow the *Bismarck* to prowl the Atlantic unchallenged. They immediately sent two great ships of their own out to get her. The British ships were the giant battle cruiser *Hood* and the battleship *Prince of Wales.* They were accompanied by six destroyers.

These ships steamed out of Scapa Flow to look for the *Bismarck.* They found her at dawn on May 24, 1941. Within minutes, the *Prince of Wales,* the

The *Bismarck* was accompanied by the cruiser *Prinz Eugen* (below).

The British battle cruiser *Hood* (above) was sunk by the *Bismarck* and the *Prinz Eugen* during the battle on May 24, 1941.

Hood, the *Bismarck*, and the *Prinz Eugen* had leveled their guns at each other and opened fire.

The air was filled with the sounds of exploding shells. Clouds of black, evil-smelling smoke hung over the ships.

The *Bismarck* and *Prinz Eugen* zeroed in on the *Hood*. The great German guns roared. Huge shells thundered in the morning air. Suddenly, only eight minutes after the battle had begun, the *Hood* exploded. The British ship was torn in two by German shells. She sank within minutes.

The *Prince of Wales*, now outnumbered and outgunned, took several hits. She threw up a smokescreen and made her getaway. The *Prince of Wales* would have to wait for the main British fleet, which was 300 miles away. In the meantime, however, she would follow the *Bismarck* at a distance. The British did not want to lose track of the huge battleship. There had been more than 1,400 men aboard the *Hood*. Only three had survived her sinking. The British, furious, were determined to sink the *Bismarck*.

The *Bismarck* herself had not gone untouched in the battle. The *Prince of Wales* had hit her twice. Now the mighty German ship was leaking oil. She changed her course and slowed her speed. She planned to head to a French port for repairs. Following her, miles behind, were the *Prince of Wales* and two cruisers, the *Suffolk* and the *Norfolk*. The *Suffolk* was equipped with radar. Also, the British aircraft carrier *Victorious* was to steam to within 100 miles of the *Bismarck*. Then she was to send out her nine Swordfish aircraft to attack the German ship.

It was ten o'clock that night by the time the *Victorious* reached her destination. The weather was terrible, but the Swordfish took off. At first, as they flew through rough air pockets and blinding rain, they could not find the *Bismarck*. Finally, just after midnight, they spotted her.

Immediately, the torpedo bombers swooped down on the great ship. As the Swordfish began to drop their torpedoes they were attacked by the *Bismarck's* powerful antiaircraft guns. Only one of the torpedo bombs found its mark. The *Bismarck* was so heavily armored, however, that she suffered no damage. Once more, the great German ship disappeared.

The heavily armored *Bismarck* (below) was not damaged by the bombing attacks from the Swordfish aircraft on the night of May 24.

The British searched for her during the entire next day. They found nothing. Then, at 10:30 on the morning of May 26, a Catalina aircraft spotted the *Bismarck*. She was steaming along about 700 miles from the port of Brest, on the coast of France.

Once more, the British moved in on the *Bismarck*. Fifteen Swordfish took off from the aircraft carrier *Ark Royal*, which was only 40 miles away from the *Bismarck*. They dumped all their torpedo bombs down at the German ship. Two torpedoes hit. One of them did a tremendous amount of damage. When it exploded, it jammed the rudders, damaged the propeller, and ruined the steering gear.

The British did not let up. They pounded the *Bismarck* all day and all night long. One torpedo after another slammed into the giant ship.

By the following morning, May 27, two British battleships had arrived. They were the *Rodney* and the *King George V*. The two ships opened fire. For more than an hour the big British guns blasted the crippled German ship. By 10:00 A.M. the *Bismarck's*

The British battleship *King George V* (above) helped sink the *Bismarck*.

guns had stopped returning any fire. She was a burning hulk, barely afloat. Finally, the British cruiser *Dorsetshire* sent three last torpedoes slamming into the huge German ship. At 10:40 A.M. the mighty *Bismarck* went down. Only 115 of the 2,000 men on the *Bismarck* survived.

Though the sinking of the *Bismarck* was a major victory for the Allies, the Battle of the Atlantic was far from over.

In June of 1941, U-boats chased the American battleship *Texas*. Even though the ship got away, Hitler again warned his navy to leave American ships alone.

Out in the ocean—especially during the darkness of night—it was nearly impossible to tell which ships were British and which were American. Even during the day—amid the fire and smoke of battle—it was often difficult to tell the difference. There were bound to be errors. And sometimes the Germans just couldn't resist a counterattack.

Two such incidents occurred in October of 1941, nearly two months before America officially entered the war. On October 17, a German U-boat torpedoed an American destroyer, the *Kearny*. The *Kearny* had been trying to help a convoy that was being attacked by a wolf pack. The eleven men killed were the first American casualties of the war.

The second incident was more serious. On October 31, a German submarine blew the destroyer *Reuben James* out of the water. More than 100 Americans—all the officers and most of the crew—went down with the ship. The *Reuben James* was the first American naval ship sunk in the Battle of the Atlantic.

The crew of the American destroyer *Kearny* inspects the damage done by the U-boat torpedo attack.

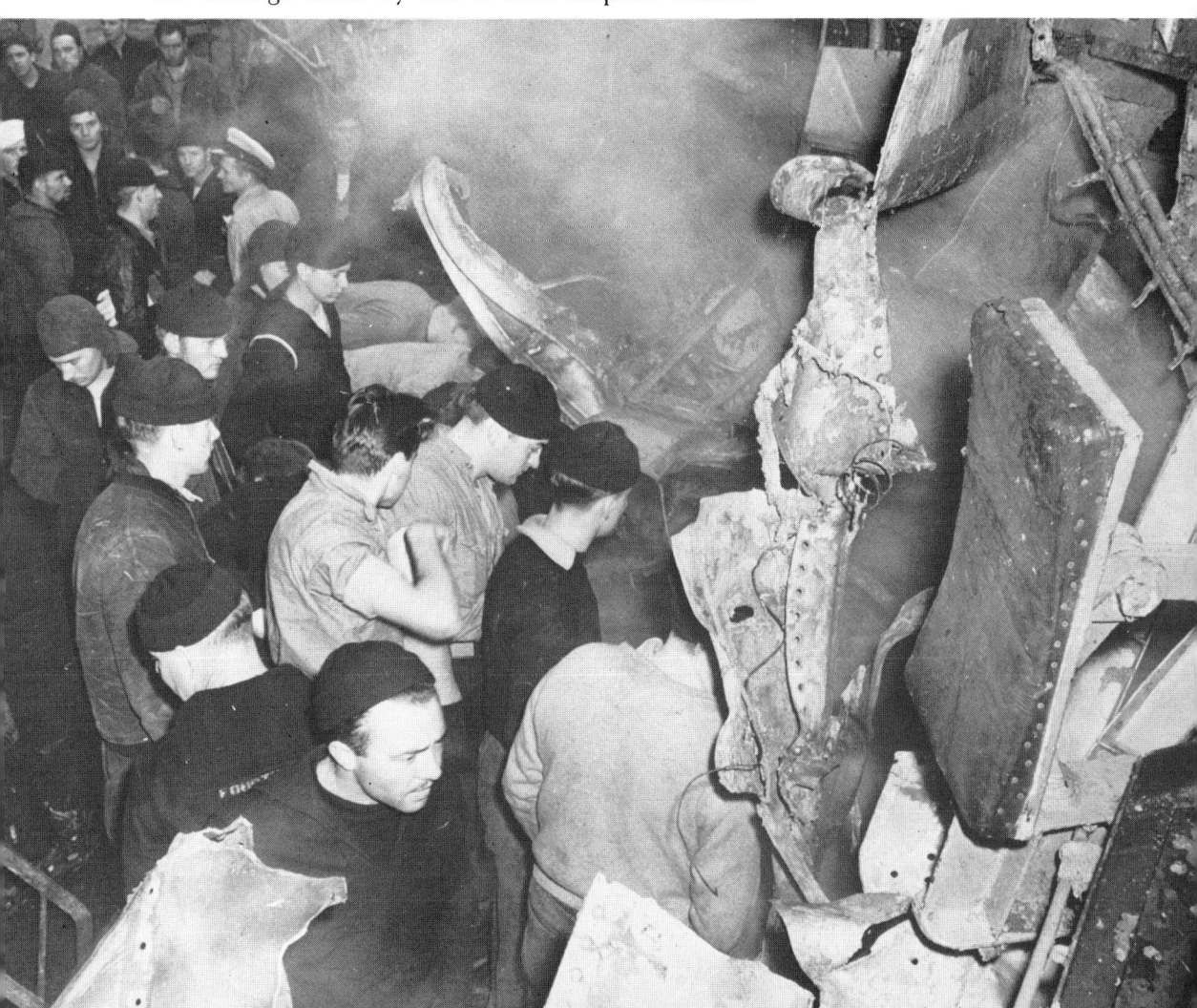

The United States tanker S.S. *Dixie Arrow* burns off Cape Hatteras, North Carolina, after being torpedoed by a U-boat on March 26, 1942.

Finally, on December 11, 1941, Adolf Hitler made the speech he had been postponing. Germany declared war on the United States. Thus, only four days after the Japanese attack on Pearl Harbor, the United States was at war with Japan, Germany, and Germany's ally, Italy.

Admiral Raeder was delighted and relieved. Now the German navy would be able to attack American ships openly. And not only escort ships in the British shipping lanes of the Atlantic. They were also free to attack American shipping on the east coast of the United States itself. Doenitz immediately began what he called Operation *Paukenschlag* (Drumroll). He unleashed his U-boats in an assault on the Americans. Eleven U-boats headed for the eastern seaboard of the United States and Canada.

The German submarines arrived on January 13, 1942. Between that date and the middle of June, the U-boats sank nearly 500 American ships. Most of these were tankers. They were carrying oil necessary for the Allied war effort.

The U-boats, as usual, stayed under the water during the day. When night came, they surfaced and picked off as many ships as possible before dawn. The U-boat commanders found it hard to believe that they encountered so little resistance. The Wolves had indeed been set loose among a herd of defenseless sheep.

The Americans were stunned. They were short of escort ships and protective aircraft. Most of these were being used in the war with Japan in the Pacific. The Americans were totally unprepared to fight this type of war on their own shore. For months they did everything wrong. Crews on merchant ships did not maintain radio silence. They frequently gave away their positions. The destroyers that did patrol the shipping lanes kept to very strict schedules. They didn't vary their routes. They didn't vary their time schedules. The U-boats knew exactly when the destroyers would be "making their rounds." During these times, of course, the submarines stayed out of sight. The rest of the time they knew they were safe.

Strangest of all perhaps, there were no blackouts of coastal cities. The government did not want Americans to panic. They tried to suppress the fact that the war had come so close to home. Also, blackouts might keep tourists—and their money—away from vacation spots. As a result, from New England to Florida, the shore was nearly as bright at night as it was during the day. Merchant ships up and down the coast, outlined against the brightness, made excellent targets. It was strange indeed to see crowds of tourists gawking at fiery naval battles in the waters off the East Coast.

A seaman aboard the oil tanker S.S. *Pennsylvania* fights a fire after the ship was struck by a torpedo from a U-boat in July of 1942.

GREENLAND

Hood

Hudson Bay

CANADA

UNITED
STATES
OF AMERICA

THE BATTLE
OF THE
ATLANTIC

Atlantic Ocean

CUBA

Caribbean Sea

Representative areas of
Allied shipping losses

Graf Spee

SOUTH AMERICA

Planes from aircraft carriers and anti-submarine coastal blimps (above) formed part of the improved air cover for convoys off the United States coast after the staggering shipping losses during the first few months of 1942.

Though the British had had years of experience in combatting the U-boats, the United States had paid very little attention to their suggestions. But the Allies could not afford to lose ships, and the supplies they carried, at this rate.

Finally, the United States began to listen to the British. Convoys were organized. Under escort, tankers and other merchant ships dashed safely from port to port. Air cover also was improved. The number of sinkings began to decrease. It became more and more difficult for the U-boats to operate.

Unwilling to waste his U-boats in this situation, Doenitz pulled them out and sent them farther south. They began to go after shipping in the Caribbean and the Gulf of Mexico. Before long, however, the Americans had organized southern shipping into convoys. This made it more difficult for the wolf packs to attack. So in July, the U-boats headed out to the middle of the Atlantic. Finally, they had left American shipping lanes. But the destruction they had caused probably set back the Allied war effort by at least a year.

A Hedgehog bomb projector (below) that fired twenty-four small bombs at a time was another weapon the Allies developed for use against the U-boats.

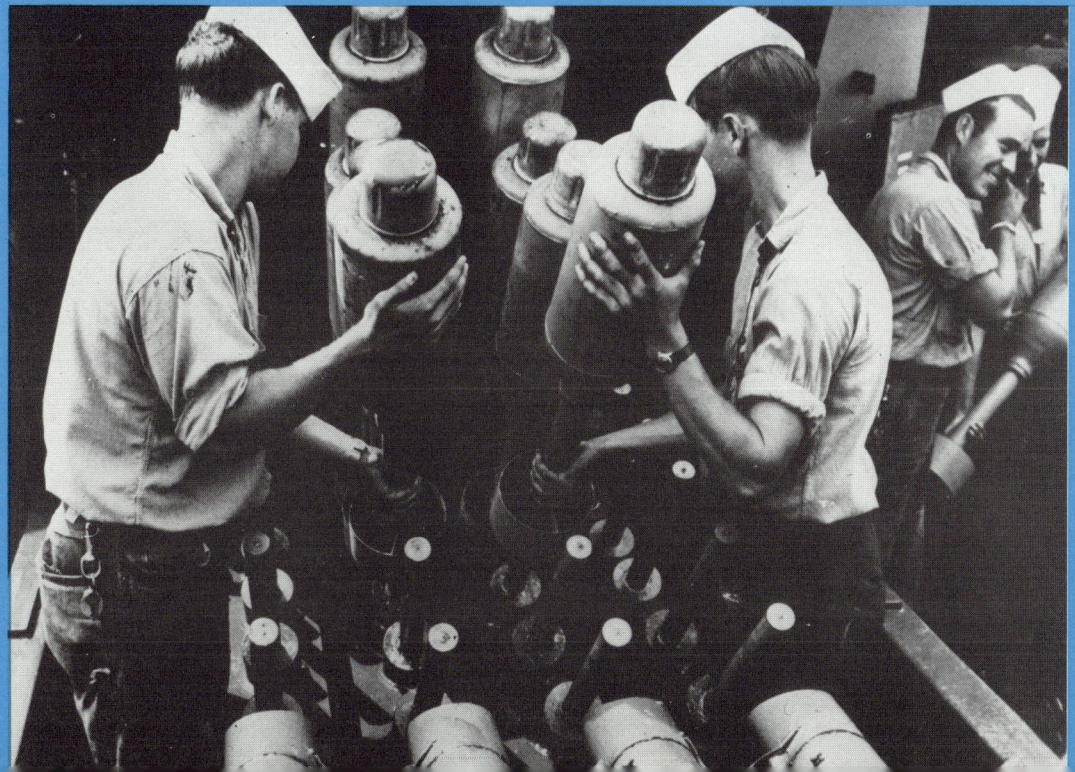

The crew of the U.S.S. *Greer*, on convoy duty in the North Atlantic, fires a gun during night action.

The U-boats were very effective in the mid-Atlantic during the last half of 1942. They kept out of the range of land-based aircraft. They attacked Allied convoys at will. Doenitz increased the size of the wolf packs. This meant that they had more torpedoes available. So each time a convoy was attacked, more ships were damaged or sunk. During 1942, German submarines destroyed more than 1,000 Allied ships.

Then came the new year—1943. The Battle of the Atlantic was about to shift. After months and months of hard work and research, everything began to come together for the Allies.

In their escort fleets, they were using faster aircraft carriers, and the newer merchant ships themselves were faster. A more effective convoy pattern was being used. New long-range planes could reach hundreds of miles into the Atlantic. The convoys were better protected than ever.

And, possibly most important of all, the Allies had finally developed a new, more effective radar. Ships and planes equipped with this improved radar were able to pinpoint the position of a U-boat almost exactly. Suddenly, U-boat losses rose sharply. The Allies were catching them totally unaware and blowing them up, one after the other. Admiral Doenitz was puzzled—and concerned. What was happening? At first, he was convinced that there was a traitor in the German navy. But none was found. Only later did he learn that radar was his enemy.

Right: Three captured U-boat crewmen shiver on the deck of a Coast Guard cutter after being fished out of the North Atlantic. Center: A U-boat under air attack. Bottom: Survivors of a German submarine await rescue by the ship that sank their U-boat.

Above: Nazi seamen on the deck of their U-boat only minutes before it sank. Twelve of these men were picked up as war prisoners.
Center: The battleship U.S.S. *Mississippi* on patrol in the Atlantic.
Bottom: Lookouts on the U.S.S. *Greer* watch merchant ships in their convoy heave in rough North Atlantic seas.

This U-boat is under attack by the Coast Guard cutter *Spencer*.

During February, March, and April of 1943, the British and Americans sank a record number of U-boats. During May, an even greater number were sunk. By the end of May, Doenitz had no choice. He was forced to pull his remaining U-boats out of the North Atlantic. As he himself wrote later, "We had lost the Battle of the Atlantic."

Even so, Doenitz went back to the North Atlantic in September of 1943. It was a mistake. He continued to lose U-boats at an alarming rate.

For all practical purposes, the Allies had won the Battle of the Atlantic in 1943. Though fighting would continue into 1944 and 1945, much had changed. The terrifying U-boat wolf packs would never again be effective. Nor would the mighty German surface ships such as the *Bismarck*.

The Allies were in control of the Atlantic. Over these shipping lanes would flow more and more and larger and larger convoys. Supplies, troops, vehicles, weapons, and ammunition would all be brought together for the major effort of the war in Europe. D-Day, the invasion of Normandy, was to take place on June 6, 1944. That invasion, and the ultimate end of World War II, could not have taken place if the Atlantic had not been made safe for Allied shipping.

Huge convoys such as this one brought supplies and troops safely across the Atlantic in 1943, 1944, and 1945.

A motor torpedo boat on patrol duty off the British coast.

INDEX

About the Author

A native of Alabama, G.C. Skipper has traveled throughout the world, including Jamaica, Haiti, India, Argentina, the Bahamas, and Mexico. He has written several other children's books as well as an adult novel. Mr. Skipper has also published numerous articles in national magazines. He is now working on his second adult novel. Mr. Skipper and his family live in North Wales, Pennsylvania, a suburb of Philadelphia.